BANBURYSHIRE
IN OLD PHOTOGRAPHS

Happy Birthday Roy
from Ken and Cynthia
24/4/92

BANBURYSHIRE
IN OLD PHOTOGRAPHS

COLLECTED BY
MELISSA BARNETT & SARAH GOSLING

ALAN SUTTON
1988

Alan Sutton Publishing Limited
Brunswick Road · Gloucester

First published 1988

British Library Cataloguing in Publication Data

Banburyshire in old photographs.
1. Oxfordshire. Banbury region, history
I. Gosling, Sarah II. Barnett, Melissa
942.5'73

ISBN 0-86299-412-8

Typesetting and origination by
Alan Sutton Publishing Limited.
Printed in Great Britain by
WBC Print Limited.

CONTENTS

INTRODUCTION

Banburyshire (a term used since at least the 1830s) is not an area recognised on any map and its boundaries do not coincide with any political or administrative limits. It is not even all within Oxfordshire but includes parts of Warwickshire and Northamptonshire as well. The area possesses nonetheless a distinct identity, beyond the purely practical links of all its villages to Banbury as their market town centre.

This regional character is less marked in the 1980s, but some elements of the subtle blend are still in evidence – the colours and shapes of the landscape, traditional building styles and materials, a diluted regional accent and dialect. Much else that made Banburyshire different has disappeared, from distinctive farming practices to horse-drawn Oxfordshire wagons and the village craftsmen who provided and repaired tools, vehicles and harness for local farmers.

Photographs, and books such as Flora Thompson's *Lark Rise to Candleford* and M.K. Ashby's *Joseph Ashby of Tysoe*, are among the more vivid and direct sources available for the study of the last hundred years in Banburyshire. They provide powerful images of the process of change, but it is important not to fall into the nostalgia trap of references to a 'vanished world'. The rapid and large-scale changes of this century have not happened within a timeless framework of static rural life or traditions. Change and evolution have always been constant elements of the regional traditions of Banburyshire, although they have usually come about at a slower pace.

So, what is distinctive about Banburyshire? The most basic abiding factor has been the underlying local geology. The character of the region is created by the colours and forms of the landscape. Between the limestone country of mid-Oxfordshire and the Warwickshire clay vale lie the small hills of the north Oxfordshire Redlands which are the essence of Banburyshire. The underlying marlstone rocks slope towards the south-east, from the high scarp cliffs of Edgehill towards a gentler and less dramatic landscape. The rocks are cut through by the valleys of streams flowing south and east towards the River Cherwell. These valleys, of the Sor Brook and the River Swere, create an undulating small-scale landscape, with only occasional long vistas. The Redlands continue north-east of Banbury towards Northampton, with the more open valley of the Cherwell flowing south to join the Thames at Oxford.

Banburyshire's rusty-brown ironstone villages are strung along the river and stream valleys, on sites where dry ground and good water supplies are combined. Today they still show the building styles and materials of three centuries ago – the local ironstone with roofs of straw thatch. New materials were available from the late eighteenth century – brickyards were set up along the canal between Cropredy and Deddington, and blue Welsh slate was imported – but bricks remained expensive, being used only for the grander buildings like chapels, schools and a few new farms. There was little housebuilding in the countryside until the present century, by which time the local stone was a costly choice and most of the local brickyards were gone.

The soils of Banburyshire have given rise to one of the most fertile farming regions in Europe. Farming has always been the area's wealthiest industry and, until modern times, the biggest employer of labour. In 1809, Arthur Young, surveying the agriculture of Oxfordshire, described the Redlands soil as 'the glory of the county. It is deep, sound . . . and adapted to every plant that can be trusted to it.' The proportions of the products of this mixed farming economy – grain, sheep, cattle and horses – have varied with market prices, but the basic underlying pattern was traditionally one of arable crops on the higher ground, with grazing for sheep and cattle on the steeper slopes and in the valleys.

The photographic record largely dates from a period of stagnation in Banbury-shire farming. After a period of good yields and high profits starting in the 1830s, times changed from the 1870s, as imported foreign grain and meat, along with poor harvests, created a severe depression. Many farmers went out of business and many farm labourers emigrated to Canada or Australia. The rural population declined dramatically. Farming did not recover, and therefore the pace of change was slow, until after the Second World War.

The village tradesmen and craftsmen shown in these photographs are largely those dependent on the needs and the products of this old pattern of local farming. Before the tractor and the motor vehicle, horses were vital: to pull ploughs, carts and wagons on the farm, and for local and long-distance transport. Blacksmiths, farriers, harness-makers and saddlers were equally essential. The photographs of the plushweavers of Shutford also depict the end of a long tradition of weaving, based on a local farming product – wool. For a century from 1750, plush was the best-known product of Banbury and its villages. At its peak, 70 per cent of all English plush was made in Banburyshire. Banbury was the collecting, finishing and marketing centre for handloom weavers in many local villages, whose plush pieces were sent for furnishings, clothing and servants' liveries in England, Europe and beyond. After the closure of the last Banbury firm in 1909, Wrench's Shutford plush mill was the only manufacturer in the world of hand-woven livery plush, until it too closed in 1948.

The twentieth century has brought dramatic changes in local shopping habits and patterns. Victorian Banbury has been called the 'metropolis' of the carrier's cart, at the centre of an intricate trading and transport network which linked the town to a hinterland of 150 nearby towns and villages through the (at least) weekly carriers. An increasing range of goods was available through the market town, but much day-to-day purchasing was still of village products, hence the photographs of a Deddington shoemaker and a Steeple Aston bakery. With the coming of buses in the 1920s, more village people travelled to town, for shopping, for leisure or for work. The more recent growth in private car ownership is again changing shopping horizons. What will a similar book of photographs in 50 years' time show as the effects on Banburyshire villages of the coming of the M40 motorway?

Local economic links and industrial patterns were altered by two earlier transport revolutions the effects of which fall within the scope of these photographs – the Oxford Canal from 1778 and the railway network from the 1850s. The photographs of the canal, all taken early this century, show almost the end of its use for the bulk transport of heavy goods – coal, pig-iron, slate and tar from the Midlands, and Banburyshire grain, hay, straw, malt and beer to London and Birmingham – which finally ceased in the 1930s. The canal's chief economic impact was on Banbury itself, stimulating the town's industries and emphasising its role as a distribution centre for the rural hinterland. The Oxford–Birmingham railway from 1850 followed the same route along the Cherwell valley and competed directly with the Oxford Canal. In contrast, the Banbury to Kingham section of the Cheltenham line, opened in 1887, swung south-west through Adderbury, Bloxham and Hook Norton and spread its effects more widely. For a few decades, the quarrying of the ironstone in these villages for low-grade iron ore became a viable proposition.

This book is not, however, intended to act as a serious introduction to Banburyshire's history, for two good reasons. This is an area which supports active, increasing (and publishing) local history studies and societies; the other available sources are legion. In addition, among the many qualities of historic photographs is that of the simple aesthetic pleasure of a strong and arresting image. Many of these Banburyshire photographs have been included for that reason.

The compilers of this volume have been of necessity highly selective; there are thousands of eligible photographs. The choice is in the end partly a personal one, but the range, in date and subject, of available photographs has also played a part. Images dating from before 1900 are rare, limited largely to studio portraits of village people by market-town photographers in Banbury or Bicester, or to the work of London photographers, as in the case of the elegant group near Adderbury church in the 1850s. The albums of Bloxham School have preserved an exceptional group of early photographs of that village.

With the arrival of the postcard boom from around 1905, the trickle of local images becomes a flood. This selection draws heavily on the preserved glass plate negatives and postcards of three main firms: Packer Studios of Chipping Norton, B.R. Morland and a predecessor of Blinkhorn's, both of Banbury.

The Packer Studio's archive images continue through until after the Second World War. For the mid-century the professional images have been supplemented by some valuable and less formal family albums, reflecting the explosion of camera ownership and use.

The compilers of this selection of Banburyshire photographs have both a professional interest in the subject, as past and present curators of Banbury Museum, and a shared affection and enthusiasm for the region and its photographs. We hope that this book will encourage more people to offer their local photographs for preservation or for copying by the museum but, more importantly, that readers will enjoy the images of Banburyshire that we have chosen.

Villages

THE LANE, TADMARTON. 356.

A BANBURYSHIRE COTTAGE ROW, probably built in the late eighteenth century, using the locally available ironstone and thatch. The three nearer chimneys are of red brick, a material whose use in village houses became more frequent in the nineteenth century. On this quiet lane, set at right angles to the main village street, geraniums are planted in pots by the front doors.

A HORSE-DRAWN THRESHING DRUM in a quiet street in Shutford before the First World War. The road surface is not yet of tarmac, but of pounded limestone, dusty in late summer heat as here, and muddy in winter.

A COVERED HORSE-DRAWN CARRIER'S CART passing through Wardington, north of Banbury, around 1910.

THE RICH TEXTURE, if not the colour, of Banburyshire villages. This is Barford St Michael in the 1920s.

AN UNFAMILIAR ANGLE on the large and prosperous village of East Adderbury, looking north-east along the High Street past the stores and the Royal Oak in the early years of this century. This central part of the village, around St Mary's Church, has the intricate, almost jumbled, layout of long organic growth. The field in the background will be the site of the neat, rectangular streets of the Twyford Garden Estate along the Banbury–Oxford road in the 1920s.

A LEISURELY SCENE with a daytime population of women and children outside the New Inn, Horley, around 1910.

CHILDREN DRAWING WATER, The Green, Swalcliffe, in the 1930s. This was not a task set up especially for the photographer; most village homes were still without piped water. Their school is the low, pantiled building at the top of the picture.

WILLIAM JOHNSON'S LOCAL DELIVERY TROLLEY in Barford. 1920s.

THE IRONSTONE HOUSES AND FLOURISHING GARDENS of the small village of Swerford, on the south-western edges of the Banbury region, photographed in the 1920s.

A SUNNY SUMMER'S DAY in Milcombe around 1910. In the foreground is Horace Tibbett's blacksmith's shop and further down the street are two groups of girls, one carrying a load of hay on her head.

LOOKING DOWN THE HIGH STREET in East Adderbury towards St Mary's church and the former tithe barn of New College, Oxford, before the First World War. The splendid new pavement contrasts with the limestone road surface of the days before regular motor traffic.

THE MAIN OXFORD–BANBURY ROAD, New Street, Deddington in the 1930s. The telegraph poles were new additions to the village street scene, but the pump on the left was still in use. The garage on the corner of Hudson Street is still (1988) in operation, to serve vastly increased motor traffic. It would be difficult to find an opportunity to photograph this empty street today.

THE LOWER END of the village of Alkerton in the valley of the Sor Brook north-west of Banbury. Before the First World War.

THE GREEN. SHENINGTON. K.

ON THE OTHER SIDE OF THE SOR BROOK lies the village of Shenington. The trees on the Green provided some welcome shade for the children.

LOOKING DOWN ON HORNTON from the steep valley side, around 1910. The village houses and farms are typical of the traditional style and materials of Banburyshire buildings – locally-quarried rich red ironstone and plain, thatched roofs.

The Land

GEORGE BODFISH, SHEPHERD at Sibford Grounds Farm in the 1880s, with his flock of Oxford Down sheep. On the windy uplands he sensibly wears an overcoat over his smock.

SHEARING SHEEP BY HAND (above) at the turn of the century in Heyford and (left) the beginnings of mechanisation with a Lister engine some twenty years later. Although sheep rearing has never been as important in Banburyshire as in the neighbouring Cotswolds, sheep have formed an important element in the mixed farming economy and some farmers have maintained large flocks, particularly in the Cherwell valley south of Banbury.

LADEN HAY WAGONS at harvest time in Aynho (above) and at Lawn Farm, Cropredy (below) before the First World War. Note the stocks to the left on the above photograph.

IRA GILKES, FARMER, in the 1880s. He was born into a long-standing north Oxfordshire family in Swalcliffe, and farmed four fields there. He later moved to Street Farm, until his death in 1925.

LEFT: EMMA GILKES, widow of Ira, leasing (gleaning) in the 1930s. She had come to the village in service with the Norris family of Swalcliffe Park. She went leasing partly out of habit and partly to feed a few chickens while living with her daughter in old age. Below: The Gilkes family outside Street Farmhouse, Swalcliffe, around 1910. From the left, Fred Mobbs, an orphan cared for by the Gilkes, who was killed in the First World War; Emma Gilkes; Lizzie and Georgina, her daughters; Jesse, her son, who later enlisted in the Canadian Mounties.

BUILDING A RICK at Manor Farm, Hethe, at the end of the nineteenth century. Two men are standing in the 'pitching hole' to pass the hay from the wagon to the top of the rick.

A WELCOME REST after putting out a rick fire in the fields of Swalcliffe Park in 1928. From the left: William Webb, Arthur Nicholls, Roland Eeley, Horace Gilkes, Ross Gilkes, William Gilkes, Frank Lines, Will Smith.

WOMEN WERE OFTEN EMPLOYED to help bring in the harvest. Here they are raking hay in Bloxham in the 1880s.

MEN, BOYS AND HORSES TAKE A REST from harvesting hay with a sail reaper in Fringford, 1880s.

A REAPER BINDING at Williamscote near Wardington, 1898.

A FINE CROPREDY-MADE WAGON, traditionally painted in yellow and red, in use for the hay harvest at Kilby's farm, Great Bourton, around 1910.

TOM BOSWELL, CARTER, who worked with the horses on Manor Farm, Cropredy.

TRACTOR POWER on Mr Woolgrove's farm in Barford in 1943. This photograph is taken from *Twenty Four Square Miles*, an important film record of life in the villages south and west of Banbury. The area was taken as a sample of the English countryside, to examine its problems and to recommend policies for reconstruction after the Second World War.

BUILDING A RICK on Jack Stephen's Manor Farm, Twyford, after the Second World War. Four o'clock tea is brought out for Eric Smith (on the tractor), Lionel Golding and Burt May (behind the tractor).

THE THRASHING DRUM on Manor Farm, Twyford, before 1950. The straw was trussed by the machine and raised into the rick with an elevator.

THE BRAND NEW COMBINE HARVESTER at work on the Manor Farm, Twyford, in 1951.

JOAN CAVE, A LAND ARMY GIRL from Tadmarton, raking with Duke in the shafts, again at Manor Farm, during the Second World War.

A THRASHING DRUM powered by a massive steam engine, on the farm of H.O. Bennett in Shenington in 1919. To offset the cost of such expensive equipment, it was also hired out to other local farmers.

GEORGE NEWMAN has brought in the cows for milking at Manor Farm, Thenford in 1949. Cattle rearing played a part in the mixed farming of Banburyshire but larger scale dairy farming has mainly been concentrated on the meadowlands of the Cherwell valley.

UNTIL THE ESTABLISHMENT of the purpose-built cattle market in Grimsbury in 1925, cattle were sold in the streets of Banbury. This is the aptly named Cowfair in the 1920s, on market day, with one of the new Midland Red Buses in front of the Town Hall.

Church and Chapel

IN THE VICARAGE GARDEN in Adderbury a group of elegantly dressed visitors pose for the London photographers, Dolamore & Bullock, in the 1850s.

Beside the splendours of the three best-known churches of Banburyshire – Bloxham, Adderbury and Kings Sutton – there is a rich legacy of smaller ironstone village churches as here in Wigginton, around 1910.

TWO LONG-SERVING LOCAL VICARS who played important roles in wider village life at the turn of the century. Both were involved in the schooling, clubs and societies of their respective parishes. Right: Revd Blythman, Vicar of Shenington for 57 years from 1869 to 1926, and of Alkerton from 1900 to 1926.

Below: Revd Henry Gepp of Adderbury (1874–1913), pictured outside his Vicarage.

BODICOTE WESLEYAN SUNDAY SCHOOL CHILDREN in 1910.

PROMINENT MEMBERS of the Anglican congregation in Cropredy in 1902. Standing, from left: J.J. Bonner (headmaster); G.T. Amos (farmer); Thomas Cooknell (shoemaker); Robert Smith (builder); James Gilbert (basket and chairmaker); Edward Wayte (Prescote Manor); Charles Gardner (plumber and decorator); W.J. Lambert (farmer); Alfred Smith (builder). Seated: R.A. Chesterman (farmer); William Anker (farmer); Major James Slack; Mr Wayte sen. (Prescote Manor); George Griffin (farmer).

THIS EDWARDIAN VIEW OF SWALCLIFFE from the west is dominated by two splendid and linked buildings: the Church of SS Peter and Paul, whose nave was built before the Norman Conquest, and the rectorial tithe barn built in the early fifteenth century for William of Wykeham's, New College, Oxford.

THE TITHE BARN IN ADDERBURY, again very close to the church, was also built for New College Oxford, in the fourteenth century. The remaining bays were converted into a stable by Lord Haldon in 1877. He put in the two dormer windows seen in this view of about 1910.

WARDINGTON CHURCH PATH, August 1898.

HOLY TRINITY CHURCH, SHENINGTON, photographed around 1900, during the three weeks at Whitsun when the church is strewn with grass. This custom, still observed, was first recorded in 1720.

A METHODIST COLPORTEUR (possibly Mr Hillier) selling his improving wares in Tadmarton, around 1910. He was a well-known figure in Banburyshire, travelling on a large tricycle.

THE MAGNIFICENT WESTERN TOWER AND SPIRE of the medieval church of St Mary, Adderbury, set on rising ground above thatched cottages and gardens in this view of about 1905. The spire is celebrated in a local rhyme: 'Bloxham for length/ Adderbury for strength/ And King's Sutton for beauty.'

Trades

FARMING MACHINERY, a plough and a fine two-wheeled cart outside the Wardington wheelwright's shop in 1915.

TWO OF THE OXFORDSHIRE WAGONS made in the Cropredy woodyard, with wheelwrights John Green (left) and Frank Sumner (right). The wagon for Avon Old Farms was made in 1927 and that for T.W. Dunn some twenty years later. The wagons were painted in the yard in the distinctive Oxfordshire colours of yellow and red, picked out with black iron work. The signwriter, Tommy Hitchman, spaced out the lettering using a bar of soap.

THE FORGE IN FRINGFORD with foreman, smiths and interested boys, in the 1890s. The forge was attached to the post office, both then owned and run by the formidable Mrs Whitton. In 1891, Mrs Whitton took on a new post office assistant, 14-year-old Flora Timms, later celebrated as Flora Thompson, author of *Lark Rise to Candleford*. Although her portrait of life in Candleford Green is not a direct image of Fringford, much of the description is based on the character of Mrs Whitton and on her experiences in Fringford Post Office in the early 1890s.

THE SIBFORD BLACKSMITH at work. Mr
Walker was also the parish overseer.

THE CROPREDY SMITHY on the south side of the Green, around 1910. Gardner Godson, the
baker, holds the horse for the farriers Andrew Taylor and Sidney Watts, who in 1912 both
decided to emigrate to Manitoba, Canada.

AS HIS ADVERTISEMENT BROCHURE SHOWS, W.F. Hayden was a Banbury-based shoeing smith, who gave farriery classes in the surrounding countryside during the 1920s and 1930s. His forge in Castle Street West was the last to close down in Banbury.

JOHN HAYDEN & SON

F.W.C.F.

PRIZE FARRIERS

" GENERAL SMITHS

" OXY-ACETYLENE WELDERS

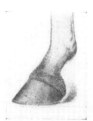

The Old Original

SHOEING FORGE

CASTLE STREET WEST, BANBURY

IN THE INTERWAR YEARS, many blacksmiths adjusted to new transport technology. Here, a group of local smiths attend a demonstration of welding outside Bloxham National School in 1923. T.G. Stevens of Bloxham is in the light coat.

A PORTRAIT OF THE ALLITT FAMILY, wheelwrights and carpenters of Adderbury, in 1904. The older child has a beautiful and no doubt home-made horse and cart.

BUTLER'S BLOXHAM WOODYARD, in the 1890s. In its heyday in the mid-nineteenth century, up to 40 men worked in this woodsawing business, started by James Butler who had brought his skills from Worcestershire. After the closure of the yard in 1902, the field was given to the village and became a recreation ground.

THE LAST SADDLER IN NORTH OXFORDSHIRE, George Elliot (right and below). George served a four-year apprenticeship in Moreton-in-Marsh before starting his own business. Lame since birth, he found the occupation suited him. He proved a popular character and his workshop was filled floor to ceiling with bags, bridles and other leather goods. The decline in the saddlery trade led him to produce all kinds of leather goods, and he was able to add 'Saddler, etc.' to the sign above the shop.

JAMES BANES, SHOEMAKER AND SHOEMENDER, at work in Deddington around 1910. Some of his family are included in the photograph because his workshop was also his home. His shop stood at the top end of Philcote Street in a row of mid-Victorian brick and slate houses more typical of the market town of Banbury. Not every village could support a shoemaker but Deddington had, and still has, some of the functions of a small market town.

QUARRYING THE IRONSTONE at the Edgehill stone quarries around 1910. Because of the longstanding quarrying trade in the nearby village of Hornton, the rich blue, purple and brown ironstone, whatever its source, is often known as 'Hornton stone'. The last Hornton stonepit closed in 1942 and the Edgehill Quarry is the last surviving producer.

NOAH CLIFTON, STONEMASON, and his sons, sinking the Cumberford well in Bloxham before the First World War. The Cliftons had been in the same trade in the village for two centuries, a continuity in marked contrast to today's family and employment patterns. Noah had six sons, all stonemasons, with the consistently Biblical names of Shem, Elijah, Amos, Eli, Daniel, and Isaac.

THE MEN WHO BUILT THE NEW HOUSES in The Rise, Twyford, for Banbury RDC in the 1920s. The council had a good reputation for the quality of its maintained houses, including those in the newly-built crescent in the background.

GILLETT'S BROUGHTON ROAD BRICKYARD, on the outskirts of Banbury: workers photographed with their children in the 1920s. This is almost at the end of the local brickmaking era, before the Banburyshire yards gave in to competition from industrially produced bricks, particularly from Bedfordshire.

BELOW: skilled woodcarvers employed by Franklin's, builders, of Deddington, proudly pose outside Fetherstone House in 1895 wearing the white linen aprons of their trade. The apprentices wore bell-boy style hats to distinguish them from the qualified woodcarvers. Mr Hall the foreman is on the far right of the photograph. From the mid-nineteenth century Franklin's produced splendid carved screens, pulpits, lecterns and choir stalls for local Oxfordshire churches and for a wider market. The photograph on the right shows a rood screen made in Deddington, erected in Franklin's yard in 1915 before being dismantled for shipment across the world to Hobart Cathedral in Tasmania. Franklin's closed down in 1917.

ELLEN JARVIS MAKING PILLOW LACE outside her home in Charity Cottages, Souldern. Lacemaking provided some badly paid but home-based employment for women, particularly in the villages bordering on Buckinghamshire. By the time photographic techniques were available to record the process, from the 1890s, very few women still made lace and the rare photographs are of older lacemakers, the last before the recent revival of the craft.

JOE ALCOCK, A PLUSH WEAVER who worked on a handloom at home in Sibford, producing cloth for W. Wrench and Sons of Shutford. Wrench's mill was the last in what was an important trade in Banburyshire at the beginning of the nineteenth century, producing velvet-like fabrics in all colours of the rainbow. These were exported all over the world.

FINISHING SILK PLUSH IN SHUTFORD: one of the last processes was to beat the damp fabric with flexible canes on a board called the 'nelly', to even the pile. It was a job for two strong men, and the sound echoed throughout the village, 1905–10.

THE SILK PLUSH POWER LOOMS in Wrench's Shutford Mill, around 1910. Stanley Wrench is in the foreground, weaver Simon Griffin at work. The business gradually declined after a disastrous fire in 1913, and finally closed down just after the Second World War.

GEORGE EAVES OF WILLIAM-SCOTE near Wardington, pictured in his ropewalk in 1898. Long individual fibres were twisted together to make ropes and cords, vital both to the farming economy and for boatmen on the Oxford Canal.

A LESS TRADITIONAL TEXTILE TRADE – a small knitting factory set up in Alkerton by H.O. Bennett from 1917 to 1922. He imported skills and techniques from Leicestershire and employed local girls to make mainly jumpers.

Sports and Fun

Text within image: TRAITOR'S FORD NEAR SIBFORD. 105.

PADDLING on a summer's day between the wars.

MAY DAY for the children of Swerford School in 1934. Myrtle Monday is the May Queen and their teacher, Miss Naylor, has helped them to make a May Garland.

THE TRADITIONAL MAY DAY MAYPOLE DANCE, merged into the celebrations for Empire Day (24 May). Adderbury, 1952.

HOOK NORTON CARNIVAL celebrations for the coronation of George V in 1910. At this time the railway viaduct on the Banbury–Cheltenham railway was still a notable landmark.

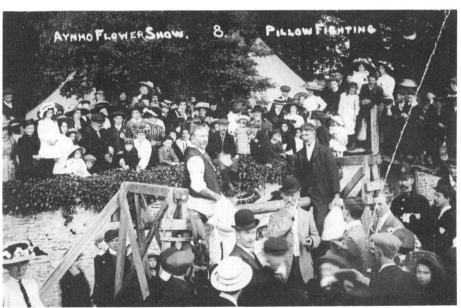

AYNHO FLOWER SHOW: Pillow fight. On the left is Constable Leatherland, stationed nearby at Croughton. The photograph was taken in 1908.

FOUR IMAGES OF SIBFORD FÊTE in August 1909, photographed by B.R. Morland of Banbury.

LORD NORTH OF WROXTON ABBEY, around the time of his 90th birthday in 1926. His lordship continued to hunt with his favourite basset hounds into old age, finally from the back of a horse-drawn trap.

THE WARWICK HUNT meet at Wroxton Abbey, home of Lord North, around 1910.

THE BICESTER HUNT on the Green, Cropredy, around 1910.

THE HEYTHROP HUNT meet in Deddington Market Place between the wars.

A PICNIC EXCURSION at Sibford School. Robert Oddie (Headmaster) is standing at the front. Note the girls wearing straw 'banger' hats. Summer 1891.

AN EDWARDIAN PICNIC PARTY in a Banburyshire park. 8 June 1908.

THIS FINE STEAM LAUNCH, the *Firefly*, was built by Henry Warriner of The Grove, Bloxham, in 1841. He was a talented and inventive engineer who also built a windmill at The Grove. The *Firefly* often sailed on the Sor Brook later in the nineteenth century, when this photograph was taken.

BOYS FISHING WITH HOME-MADE RODS in the canal, Somerton.

EDWARDIAN TENNIS PLAYERS, from an album at Bloxham School.

EATING TREACLE BUNS in the park at Adderbury House, 1937.

ADDERBURY FOOTBALL CLUB, Shipston Shield winners in 1937.

SWERFORD FOOTBALL CLUB in 1924–5.

BLOXHAM 'NIGGERS' c. 1929. Their faces were blackened as a relic of the masked mummers, a tradition which had ended by the First World War. On Boxing Day the group would perform all day around the village, collecting pennies in the tambourine. Left to right: Bill Preedy (Bumper Jones) with tambourine; Bert Green (Sally) with melodeon; Syd Charles (Uncle Neddy) with bones.

SOULDERN VILLAGE BAND OF HOPE founded by Miss Sarah Hill, owner of Woodcote. Men (left to right): James Fox, Tom Tomkins, John French, Bert Westbury, Joe Bates, Henry Bates, Robert Lake, Oliver Westbury, Will Lett, Alf Hitchman and Nathan Jarvis. Ladies (left to right): Lou Mold, Rose French, Emily Hitchman, Sarah Hill, Harriet Reeve, E. Bates, -?-.

Houses and Great Estates

'BENNETTS' IN BLOXHAM, a traditional Banburyshire yeoman farmhouse of the seventeenth century, photographed in the 1870s. It was named for the family in occupation around 1800 but, by the time of the photograph, Charles Townsend, head gardener at Bloxham School, lived there. His gardening skills are evident in the thriving patch of vegetables in front of the house.

FETCHING WATER from the Old Well in Tadmarton at the beginning of the century.

QUEENS SQUARE, BLOXHAM: George Mawle in 1923 outside his tiny cottage, demolished as part of the slum clearance scheme of 1938. In retirement he lived in the cottage with his daughter. Stairs to two bedrooms within the roof led up from the single ground floor room, heated by a large open fire. Water came from a communal tap in the square.

A SUPERB EXAMPLE of the Banbury regional style – a seventeenth-century thatched, ironstone farmhouse in Tadmarton. At the time of the photograph, probably during the 1920s, the house was remarkably unaltered, retaining a single-storey thatched bread oven.

MR AND MRS RICHARD SUMNER outside their home next to their woodyard in High Street, Cropredy.

CHARITY COTTAGES in Souldern. These may have been built to house canal workers around the turn of the nineteenth century. Here Bert Titcomb is seen outside the cottages with his bread cart. The rent for the cottages was 1s. 6d. per week.

DRAYTON, row of cottages. 1908.

THE GREAT HALL of Broughton Castle, generously furnished in the Edwardian taste. The sofas are covered with patterned Shutford plush. The fourteenth-century castle, the seat of Lord Saye and Sele, was let to tenants during this period and became the family's residence again in 1912.

Mʳ FRANK LASCELLES AT HOME   SIBFORD GOWER ... NO 1

THE EXTRAORDINARY HOME in Sibford Gower of Frank Lascelles, pageant master of the Oxford Historical Pageant, June 1907. The Manor, of no great antiquity, was formed by linking and extending several old cottages. A square tower was built on in 1908.

DEDDINGTON MANOR: two gardeners mowing the immaculate lawns, possibly as early as the 1880s.

A HORSE-DRAWN LAWNMOWER in Sibford Gower, around 1910. The mower was supplied by Samuelson's Britannia Ironworks in Banbury.

GEORGE CARTER, coachman and groom to Captain Keyser of Cotefield house (between Adderbury and Bodicote) before the First World War.

THE HOUSEHOLD STAFF at Wroxton Abbey around 1910. The central figure is the house-keeper, Mrs Cobb. The footman still wears a powdered wig.

The north Oxfordshire contribution to the Garden City movement. The tea garden on the Twyford Garden Estate, laid out soon after the First World War.

Schools

END OF TERM AT BLOXHAM SCHOOL, December 1932. The wagon was provided by Benjamin Heath of Bloxham. Bloxham School was founded in 1853 as a Church of England Boarding School for the sons of the professional classes, and much expanded in the 1860s by the Revd P. Egerton, curate of Deddington, 1860–8.

Girls at Play.   Sibford School.

SIBFORD SCHOOL, a large Quaker boarding school founded in 1842. Photographs from an early twentieth-century prospectus.

The Cricket Pavilion.   Sibford School.

PLAYING FIVES at Bloxham School in 1882.

BLOXHAM SCHOOL CAMERA CLUB, 1880. Three schoolmasters are shown: J.H.T. Goodwin, E. Manley and W.J.G. Bridges.

THE MUSIC CLUB at Bloxham School.

SIBFORD SCHOOL, the new workshop, 1910.

HOOK NORTON SCHOOL: domestic science classes in the 1930s.

THE CHILDREN OF SWALCLIFFE SCHOOL on the village green south of the church, in 1922. Standing (left to right): Roland Knight, Dorothy Eeley, Ena Eeley, Eric Morby, Flo Nicholls, Stella Haynes; (behind) Winnie Morby, Norman Eeley, -?-, -?-, Noah Stratford (in hat in front), Stanley Nichols (cap), Joe Stretton, -?-, Owl ?. Seated (left to right): Ethel Morby, Marjorie Haynes (hat), Daisy Diamond, Dorothy Haynes, Agnes Handsworth, Dorothy Handsworth, Ivy Jenkins, Flo Rogers, Ilma Stretton, Leslie Barber, Ruby Barber, Eva Rogers, -?-. Seated at front with hat: Helen Ashby.

THE CHILDREN OF DEDDINGTON SCHOOL in the early years of the century.

SOME DISGRUNTLED INFANTS in Bloxham in the 1890s.

THE SCHOLARS of Souldern Church of England School in 1914. The schoolmaster is James Wills and the teacher is Jeannie Ilott, who emigrated to Canada.

PRIMARY SCHOOL GARDENS known as Paddington in Milton Lane, Bloxham, 1911–12. Gilbert Rivers, Arthur Maule, T. Ravel, G. Brudnell, Ted Clarke, L. Coleman, Gilbert Clifton, B. Young, M. Smith, Laurence Horley.

SIBFORD SCHOOL in October 1904. Robert Oddie, headmaster, on the doorstep. Henry Tarver, gardener, with wheelbarrow. The trees on the left were planted to commemorate Queen Victoria's Jubilee.

People

THE MARRIAGE O

THE MARRIAGE of Miss Starkey at Bodicote.

CROWDS GATHERED to watch as Miss Leigh Hoskyn married Ronald Holbech of Farnborough Hall at St Mary's Church, Adderbury (above); and (below) her many flower-girls.

THE CANDIDATES for the Banbury constituency in the closely-fought General Election of January 1910. The result was reversed when the Hon. Eustace Fiennes was elected MP for Banbury in December of the same year.

FLORA THOMPSON, the eldest child of stonemason Albert Timms, was born in 1876 at Juniper Hill, a hamlet of Cottisford. In *Lark Rise to Candleford* she recalled her childhood and early youth in detailed descriptions of the everyday lives of her family and neighbours just before the traditional country ways were broken down by the rapid changes of this century.

QUEENIE MASSEY, lacemaker and bee-mistress in *Lark Rise*, in a studio portrait by a Bicester photographer in the early 1890s.

THE TWO OLDEST PEOPLE IN SIBFORD, taken to mark the end of the nineteenth century. These people's lives and memories may have gone back to the time of George III.

RICHARD AND REBECCA ROUTH. He was the first headmaster of the Friends' School at Sibford, from 1842 until 1880.

MR JOHN HOBBS AND HIS BELLS, 1850s. He was much sought after on all occasions and played an important part in the festivities to celebrate Queen Victoria's accession to the throne. The week of Whitsun was probably one of his busiest periods because, starting on Whit Monday, he attended the club feasts of the surrounding villages, finishing on the Friday, always at Bodicote.

WILLIAM ALLEN of Souldern, known as 'Tosh'. In his bachelor retirement he used to sit smoking his pipe all day at his cottage door near the entrance to the village, keeping a close eye on the comings and goings.

A GROUP OF ELDERLY WORKERS at the Shutford plush mills, photographed in 1924. Mrs Herodias Stanley, who always wore a hat, picked out 'bits' from the plush and sewed up the bags in which plush was packed for despatch; James Griffin, foreman; Enos Griffin, who still came to work at the age of 90, and Amos Turner, handloom weaver.

GEORGE EAVES, rope-maker, of Williamscote near Wardington, in a portrait of 1898.

FRANK JAKEMAN, carrier, of Swerford, with his son Cyril and his aunt, around 1910. Her sunbonnet is in the Banbury Museum collections.

GEORGE ELLIOT, of North Newington, the last saddler in north Oxfordshire, as a young man. The only time he was out of the saddlery trade was when he worked in Banbury during the First World War filling shells.

A RARE PORTRAIT of the photographer Percy Simms of Chipping Norton, in 1907. This oak in Wharf Lane, Souldern, was struck by lightning in that year and many local people came to see the sight.

GEORGE AND EDMUND HAWKINS, two brothers from Adderbury who were sextons at St Mary's Church well into old age. At the time of this photograph (around 1905) they were aged 92 and 94. In their youth they had been Morris dancers, and they helped to record the traditional local dances.

THEODORE LAMB from Sibford, a solitary and eccentric character who lived in a battered shack in a field on the Brailes Road from 1921 until the early 1950s. He wore tattered sacks and plastered his long hair with mud. He earned some money and food by repairing clocks and watches, until banned from Banbury for his dress. On summer Sundays for 2s. 6d. he would pose for people to take his photograph.

SECTION NINE

Shopping
and Transport

THE OLD AND NEW METHODS OF MILK DELIVERY. Horse and smart motor vehicle meet on a Banburyshire road before the First World War.

THE FAMILY OF GEORGE EAVES, ropemaker, with their pony and trap at Williamscote, around 1898.

MR HILLIER, METHODIST COLPORTEUR, travelled on his large tricycle around Tadmarton, selling his religious tracts.

MR JEFFKINS AND HIS SON delivering meat in Swerford.

MRS MARIE GODSON, wife of Gardner Godson the baker, with their horse Queenie and delivery van near Station House, Cropredy. In their bakehouse in Church Lane they made loaves, cakes and pies for delivery as far as Chipping Warden, Wardington and the Bourtons.

MOTORISED DELIVERY VANS increased village trade for the market town specialist shops. Chapman Bros. were, until the 1980s, a furnishing and removal firm in Bridge Street, Banbury.

THE BANBURY AND DEDDINGTON BUS, around 1920.

THE OLD ELM TREE BUS HALT at the crossroads in Sibford Ferris in the 1920s.

ALFRED ALLEN'S BUS outside his public house, the Bell in Shenington in 1930. The arrival of bus travel, gradually replacing the slower carriers' carts, opened up many possibilities for people in the villages to shop, to take their leisure or to commute to work in the market towns.

JOHN HAYNES' BAKERY in Bloxham, Boxing Day 1947. On Christmas Day he kept the ovens working to cook the large turkeys belonging to special customers.

THE BREAD CART outside Mr Albert Titcomb's General Stores and Bakery in Souldern around 1910. The gated entrance to the shop let air to the sausages, pies and faggots before the age of refrigeration. With the cart are the grocer's three younger sons and the pony, Nimrod.

JOE BATES, the Souldern carrier, with his van in Horsefair, Banbury, 1911. Until well into this century carriers were a vital economic link between the market town and the nearby villages. Joe Bates, for example, would fetch shopping for twopence a parcel. Banbury, the 'metropolis' of the carrier's cart, relied on the trade from 150 towns and villages on the carrier network.

VIC WESTON in Steeple Aston with the carrier's cart.

BANBURY COOPERATIVE SOCIETY, founded in 1866, expanded rapidly until it had 15 branches in nearby villages and small towns by 1915. The first village branch shop was established in Bloxham in thatched premises (above), shown here with Frank Lovegrove at the door. It was replaced in 1907 by a purpose-built brick and slate store (below).

OLD CO-OP BAKERY in Heyford Road, Steeple Aston, around 1895.

COOPERATIVE SOCIETY milk and bread delivery carts in Round Close Road, Adderbury, 1930s. Left: Vic Lynes, right: Ron West.

WROXTON, the Banbury Cooperative Society's Branch No. 4, in about 1916.

SWERFORD POST OFFICE STORES.

T.H. (TICKY) WELL'S Drapery Store, Deddington.

A WONDERFULLY WELL-STOCKED ironmonger's shop, the 'Bazaar' in Hook Norton in the early years of the century.

BONE-SHAKERS at Bloxham School in the late nineteenth century.

BLOXHAM CYCLE CLUB, 1893. Centre is Mr William Bradford, the schoolmaster. Note the pennyfarthing bicycles at the back.

THERE IS NO CLUE to the identity of these early motorcyclists photographed by B.R. Morland of Banbury in 1910, but their number plate reveals Oxfordshire origins.

COTTISFORD SCHOOL: County Education Officer's car, 1902.

WITH HIS 'ORDINARY' CYCLE, this (unidentified) proud young cyclist posed for a portrait by Grimmett's Photographic Studios, Banbury, between 1883 and 1897.

SECTION TEN

Industries

THE STONE FACE of the Park Pit, Hook Norton, in the 1920s. Toppers cleared the topsoil and ran the plank with their navvy wheelbarrows. The fillers below loaded the trains with wide forks, breaking larger lumps of ironstone with a sledgehammer.

THE LOCOMOTIVE *Joan* backs on to the train as the last tub is filled with ironstone.

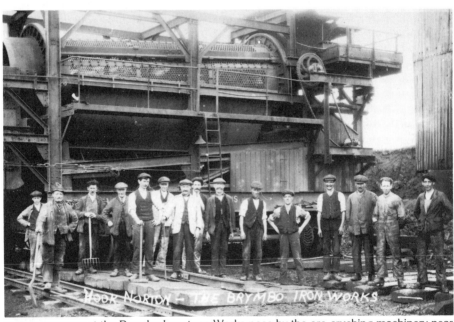

QUARRY WORKERS at the Brymbo Ironstone Works pose by the ore-crushing machinery near the calcining kilns, 1920s.

THE DUFFIELD IRON CORPORATION'S WORKS AT ADDERBURY was established like the ironstone workings at Hook Norton, as a result of the bulk transport possibilities of the Banbury–Cheltenham Railway, opened in 1887. The Adderbury works closed down shortly before the Second World War. Workers are shown below.

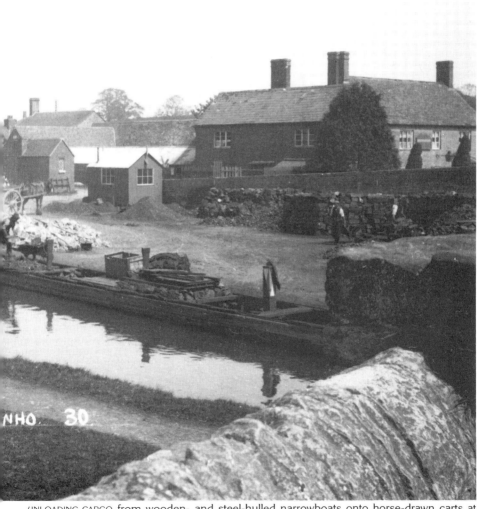

UNLOADING CARGO from wooden- and steel-hulled narrowboats onto horse-drawn carts at Aynho Wharf in the early years of this century.

A NARROW BOAT, laden with timber, moored just south of Banbury on the Oxford Canal in the 1920s. The canal reached Banbury in 1778 and became a major artery of bulk commercial traffic until the railways took away much of the trade after 1850.

NARROWBOATS on the Oxford Canal at Nell Bridge, Aynho, 1910; looking south-east towards Nell Bridge Farm. Taken in winter or early spring, with flooded water meadows between the canal and the railway.

ENJOYING THE CANAL at Aynho.

THE BANBURY AND CHELTENHAM DIRECT RAILWAY was built to connect London, the Midlands and the eastern counties with South Wales and the West, and principally for the transport of ironstone. The photograph shows the railway being built, at the cutting east of the Barford Road bridge, Bloxham, in about 1885.

BLOXHAM STATION GROUP PHOTOGRAPH, around 1925. An outside frame Dean goods locomotive stands between the barrow crossing and the South Newington Road bridge. The stationmaster is Mr Lloyd. William Clarke, the guard, holds a shunting pole and Basil Packer, the photographer's son, is on the far right.

ADDERBURY STATION on the Banbury–Cheltenham line looking east, in the 1920s.

CROPREDY GWR STATION STAFF, around 1911. Mr Thomas Miller the station-master was a stickler for order, and won prizes for the best-kept station.

MR W. HALL, linesman, photographed by a Banbury photographer in the 1880s.

WAGONS AND BARRELS belonging to John Harris, Hook Norton Brewery. In 1849 John Harris moved into a farmhouse at Scotland End in Hook Norton. In the farm's malthouse he set up in business at as maltster supplying small brewhouses in the area. Eventually he built his own brewhouse and began to brew his own beer. Encouraged by his sales he enlarged the malthouse in 1865 and then in 1872 he constructed a small three-storey tower brewery mashing five quarters of malt at each brew. At one point, twelve different beers were produced. Now the present range of Best Bitter, Mild and Old Hookey is available within fifty miles of Hook Norton.

ONE OF THE HOOK NORTON BREWERY'S iron-wheeled steam wagons in 1908, built locally by the Wantage Engineering Company. Such modern forms of transport encouraged wider distribution. The steam wagon appears on the company's poster of about the same date (below) which also shows the newly-built tower brewery.

Community

WROXTON CLUB 1914. Previously the North Arms Friendly Society. Each member paid a sum
... the more they paid in, the more they got out when they were sick.

THE SOULDERN CLUB PARADE, 29 May 1909. Members took to the streets in a gay mood, carrying their staffs, with even the village schoolmaster (centre in straw hat) walking in step. The parade would have been followed by the annual feast. The three musts for the working man were firstly, a pig in the sty (every cottage, with few exceptions, had its own sty); secondly, a chain of allotment to grow enough potatoes to see his family through the year (many also grew barley to finish off the pig); and thirdly he must insure himself against illness, usually by membership of a club. The Bodicote Pig Club (below) was revived during the Second World War because of food shortages.

11.—If a Member purchase a pig which shall be proved to have been ill at the time he purchased it, and he knew of it, he shall not receive any benefit from the Society.

12.—Any Member obstructing the business of the Society at any meeting thereof shall be fined 1/-.

13.—(a) That all Members shall fill in and hand to the Secretary the proper Application Form for Rations. Failure to do this will relieve the Secretary of all responsibility to apply for Rations for such Member. All Members to supply their own bags at the time of application, for preference with name attached. All bags supplied by the Secretary will be charged at 1/- each. (b) That Members shall acquaint themselves with the delivery of Rations, and they shall collect their Rations within four days. Failure to do this renders such Member liable to a fine of 1/-, this sum to be paid for storage. No Member to remove Rations without the Secretary's permission, also for payment for their Rations.

14.—The Committee are particularly requested to show no partiality, but act honestly to all, and endeavour to the best of their judgment to give satisfaction; they will be required to investigate strictly where there is a doubt or suspicion, in order to ascertain how the case stands; if there is not sufficient proof to convict the Member, their decision must be given in his favour.

15.—All monies to be placed in the Post Office Savings Bank in the names of Three Trustees elected by the Members.

RULES AND CONTRIBUTION CARD

OF THE

BODICOTE PIG CLUB

HELD AT

THE "BAKERS' ARMS," BODICOTE

No.....................

Name ....

The object of a Club of this kind is to render assistance to those Members who through unavoidable accident or disease to their Pigs, or in case of death, do sustain loss thereby. The funds at their disposal to be derived from the Contributions of Benefit Members, and the donations of such persons as wish to promote the interest of the Society.

Established 1889

Secretary: W. H. HITCHMAN
5, East Street, Bodicote.

ADVERTISER PRESS, BANBURY.

154

THE CROWN INN, Souldern. The lady is possibly Emily Steeden, the licensee.

THE MASONS ARMS, Swerford with carrier's cart outside.

VOLUNTEER FIRE BRIGADE outside a house in Mill Street, Adderbury, 1900.

ADDERBURY FIRE CREW, around 1923, photographed in the meadow in Water Lane. Robert Beasley was the captain of the brigade and meetings were held in the Royal Oak public house in the High Street. Back row: Charlie Coleman, Harry Nelson, Albert Placket, Harry Bray; Front row: Frank Billing, Harry Bryant, Oscar Wallin, Bo Beasley, Jack Bennet, Harold Trench, Frank Flint, Fred Jones.

MRS PARRITT, Wroxton district nurse, in the 1920s.

THE SOULDERN RED CROSS at Souldern Manor around 1920. The group was formed during the early years of the First World War by the Misses Stanton of Woodcote. Back row: Miss E. Ginger, Miss S. Cox; Front row: Miss A. Bennett, Mrs England, Miss B. Kempson, Mrs Beverage.

BLOXHAM SCOUT TROOP, 1927/8. The Revd J.W. Ward, a Church Army man and curate to the Revd H.J. Riddlesdell, was scoutmaster. On the right is assistant scoutmaster Fred Mawle.

THREE MOTOR TRANSPORT WAGONS stranded on the Green, Adderbury, in April 1915. The Berkshire Express has run in 'tired Tim' with disatrous consequences.

LAYING WATER PIPES in Bloxham High Street, 1926. Mains water came to the village in 1903–4. A pumping station in Cumberford pumped water to a reservoir on Hobb Hill from which the village was supplied.

THE BRIDGE, Hook Norton on which is a Banbury Rural District Council water-cart.

LIBERAL DELEGATES in Deddington.

ACKNOWLEDGEMENTS

Banbury Museum • Bloxham School • Bloxham Village Museum
Central Office of Information • Mrs A.M. Cherry • Mrs N.M. Clifton • Barry Davies
Mr & Mrs Elliot • Mr Fox • Mr R. Hitchman • Mr & Mrs Huntriss • Mr C. Jakeman
Mr B. Jones • Mrs P. Keegan • Oxon Museum Services • Local Studies
Collections, Oxon Libraries • Mrs A. Prescott • Sibford School • Mr E. Smith
Rhoda Woodward
and our sincere thanks to all those donors who have, over the years, given their
postcards, photographs and memories to the Banbury Museum.
The photographs are not individually credited.
Banbury Museum holds information on the source of each image.